A *Windy* Day

by Robin Nelson

first step nonfiction

Lerner

Lerner Books · London · New York · Minneapolis

It is a windy day!

Can you see the wind?

We can't see the wind.

But we can feel the wind.

Wind can be strong.

Wind can be gentle.

When it is windy, sand blows.

Waves crash.

When it is windy, plants **bend.**

Seeds blow.

When it is windy,
windmills turn.

Hats blow off heads.

When it is windy, we
can **sail** in a boat.

We can ride on waves.

When it is windy, we
can fly a **kite**.

A windy day is fun!

Weather Vanes

Weather vanes are pointers that turn as the direction of the wind changes. The direction they point shows us where the wind is coming from. Weather vanes come in all shapes and sizes.

Windy Day Facts

The wind blows because cold air is heavier than warm air. Warm air rises and cold air falls. This makes wind.

Wind does not blow in a straight line. In the northern part of the world, the Earth's spinning makes wind curve to the right. In the southern part of the world, wind curves to the left.

Wind can make you feel colder. The temperature you feel when it is windy is called the windchill.

One of the windiest places on the Earth is the top of Mount Washington in New Hampshire. The wind there has been measured at 371 kilometres per hour!

The strongest winds of a hurricane can reach up to 362 kilometres per hour.

The winds of a tornado can blow more than 483 kilometres per hour.

Glossary

 bend – to change from straight to a curved shape

 kite – a covered frame that is attached to a piece of string and flown in the wind

 sail – to travel across water in a boat powered by wind

 seeds – parts of a flowering plant from which a new plant can grow

 windmills – structures that use wind power to turn a machine that grinds grain, pumps water, or makes electricity

Index

This book was first published in the United States of America in 2002.
First published in the United Kingdom in 2008 by
Lerner Books,
Dalton House,
60 Windsor Avenue,
London SW19 2RR

This edition was updated and edited for UK publication by Discovery Books Ltd., Unit 3, 37 Watling Street, Leintwardine, Shropshire SY7 0LW

Words in **bold** type are explained in the glossary on page 22.

British Library Cataloguing in Publication Data

Nelson, Robin, 1971-
    A windy day. - (First step nonfiction. Weather)
    1. Winds - Juvenile literature
    I. Title
    551.5'18

    ISBN-13: 978 1 58013 308 1

The photographs in this book are reproduced through the courtesy of: © Betty Crowell, front cover, pp. 8, 16, 19 (top right, middle and bottom left), 22 (2nd from top); © Michael S. Yamashita/ CORBIS, p. 2; © Tom McCarthy/Grant Heilman Photography, p. 3; © Chris Fairclough/Discovery Picture Library, p 4; © Francis/Donna Caldwell/Visuals Unlimited, p. 5; © Stephen Graham Photography, pp. 6, 7, 10, 22 (top); © Richard Cummins, pp. 9, 12, 13, 14, 19 (top left and bottom right), 22 (middle and bottom); © Wally Eberhart/Visuals Unlimited, pp. 11, 22 (2nd from bottom); © Michele Burgess, p. 15; © Myrleen Cate/Grant Heilman Photography, p. 17.

Printed in China